The Phoenix Living Poets

DIFFERENCES

The Phoenix Living Poets

★

DIFFERENCES

by

RICHARD KELL

CHATTO AND WINDUS

THE HOGARTH PRESS

1969

Published by
Chatto & Windus Ltd
with The Hogarth Press Ltd
42 William IV Street
London W.C.2

★

Clarke, Irwin and Co Ltd
Toronto

SBN 7011 1524 6

Printed in Great Britain by
William Lewis (Printers) Ltd Cardiff

For Muriel

Acknowledgements are due to the editors of *The Dubliner*, *The Irish Press*, *The Irish Times*, *The Listener*, *New Poetry (B.B.C.)*, *The Observer*, *Outposts*, and *Poetry Ireland*, and of the anthologies *Here Today*, *New Poems 1963*, and *My Kind of Verse*, in which many of the following poems have been published.

CONTENTS

1 : Arches

Arches on land,
half-circles only,
might dream
of what they miss.

And yet to stand
in a dark stream,
is this
not twice as lonely?

2 : The Woman

She makes no sound, no gesture;
grave and lovely in her long silk
stands waiting, and seems to understand
all that is dark to me. I draw the sword:
it glides a thread of steel across her lips,
perfecting silence. I regret
something I know must be – but it will end,
and she endure calmly.

The blade glints lethal now
to rod the prancing athlete of his head:
though he crouch wary, knife concealed,
he is no match for me. With naked breasts
the woman sits alone in her compartment.
The train moves, and we run elated –
killer and victim, two in one: myself –
effortless where she goes.

3 : *The City*

My feet slithered in mud, mashed
a lane's end slurring on the brink
of light and water. Evening shone low
its round of amber, turning pink
the clouds' edges and the snow.
The swirling river flashed.

And clear on the far side
arose the dream's manhattan, built
in piercing blocks of topaz, ruby, jade,
whose facets gleamed, whose windows spilt
unearthly light, and in my heart made
such happiness that I cried.

4 : *Oppressors*

I lie in fever, delirious. The dark bedroom
winces under the silver whip of lightning.

I write my name, my prayer for heaven's mercy,
in ropes of green smoke on the brimstone air.

Across the neat advertisements in the paper
one large and arrogant stamps itself blood-red.

The teacher says we are here to learn Egyptian:
I ask him why the hell he is talking Greek.

He drags me out to beat me. I grab, exultant.
The metre stick lands *crack* on his hardboiled head.

5 : *The Mountain*

Through the still dark I walk alone
before the moon's rising. Small winds sigh
    on grassy slopes and cliffs of stone.
Hilltops are printed black against the sky.

A gold thorn lifts behind a spur,
grows to a radiant crest that cleaves the night,
    and shines full mountain then, whose fur
is glowing wheat, is acres of combed light.

6 : *The Dedication*

I too was in the choir. Imagine! − thousands
perching along the cliffs, and then the slow
chorale descending where the water shone
at break of day. How happily alike
the music and the sea's adagio −
for we were singing to the god Poseidon.

But when the hymn was over, one by one
the singers offered prayers of dedication
and then sat down. I thought 'How very odd
that they should use this drear monastic lingo,
clammy with guilt and self-humiliation,
to honour so exuberant a god'.

The bishop then (whose cassock sheathed him snugly
against the wind and spray): *We come to thee
with contrite spirits* . . . 'But the god is gay!'
my heart protested. 'How can they not feel
the salt barbaric splendour of the sea!'
I stood there like a rock. I would not pray.

7 : *First Light*

The sun rises: dark
melts from tall buildings
   and leafy park

where a strange creature pads
whose fur is green moss
   whose form the leopard's

and trees drink deep
the quintessential calm
   of more than sleep.

8 : The Tower and the Ocean

To feel the wind up there
purling on those great battlements, I entered
the numb and stony darkness, and began to
trudge the coiled stair.

Heard, half way up, the sound
of scrubbing-brush and pail, where Mrs. Crone
worked her poor fingers to the bone
in her long daily round.

The steps were hard and cold
on which she knelt, plying her only skill
year after year, and talking gaily still
though tired and old.

No stir of life but hers. On the top floor,
roneo, box-file, desk and balance sheet
furnished a room impersonal and neat
beyond an open door.

I turned to climb — above me the sweet air,
the final twist of stone. The way was barred,
and in black letters on a card
Not Open to the Public printed there.

A loophole shone in darkness: down below,
the tennis balls were soaring, floating, and
the players reaching up in a big wind.
Their rippling tunics dazzled me like snow.

And mounds of sapphire, flaring into white,
drowned half the sky in waves
whose crumbling scarps and luminous glissades
filled all my veins with light.

Small Mercies

Someone ruled lines on a page of land
    with the railway for a margin,
and stuck the houses there in tidy rows.
Back to back or front to front, they stand
    aligned, allied, glaring
with tolerant hatred out of veiled windows.

But we are lucky, being in the end house
    of the first terrace. The back
enjoys the ramshackle remnant of a farm
turned coalyard, a meadow shared by an old horse
    and a lorry no one uses,
a tree with a night-owl hooting on its arm.

The end, of course, enjoys not being mean,
    and having its douse of air,
its glimpse of cherry branches on sky, its muddy
lane — reminds you of search and thrust, clean
    splitting, the point of vision:
headlands, the bows of ships, a man's love ready.

The Stranger

With ticking stick and boots like burst pods,
a long black overcoat and a withered hat,
a hunched hobo shuffles in our blind alley
    and sings in a loud voice.

Aria, dirge, chorale — or could it be
his own crude making? The words dissolve in wind;
only the music's warped adagio
    blares confidence in something.

And sets me wondering what weird compulsion
prods him along this road on a cramped Sunday —
the houses deadpan, the people shut away,
    not even a dog barking.

Insanity? A noisy camouflage
for a burglar quiet as a draught? Intoxication?
A drifter down on his luck. I'll give him the cash
    he needs because he needs it.

Diminuendo. I wait for him to return
doing his round of knocking. The singing stops.
He passes again, glaring from right to left . . .
    Has gone, without a sound.

And leaves me free to imagine him possessed:
that suddenly — learning of death perhaps —
he knew what he had to sing to this dead end
    in one candescent stanza.

God knows what he was at: I'm none the wiser.
But feel his ghost haunting my ear, and wish
that all of us could sing in our blind alleys
    with such a clear madness.

Microcosm

As a small wilderness
the vegetable patch
declares its worth:
let loose, the children scratch
in hollows of dried earth,
bounce on a plank, or watch
the insects in the grass,
their bodies edged with light,
the tall weeds luminous.

No more than we deserve:
they to be left alone
to play, and I to work
in this clean living-room
their mother keeps so well:
routines we may not shirk
or barely stay alive;
with skill we buy the freedom
that disciplines our skill.

Too young to think it out,
how could they know that we
who sometimes nag and shout
are free when they are free,
clear of the mean restraint
grafted in all of us:
'Keep out of range', I'd say,
'let me be generous' —
and they'd wonder what I meant.

Jazz Boat

The whispering roar of jets going over, tear-
ing slowly a sheet of silence. Clicking tongues
round mud and roots. A coolness in the air.
Where houseboats lull, a lamp's reflected light
on supple darkness floats its golden rungs.
Watching their movement in a cold black frame
of leaves, I think of Asmodeus' flight,
and fury settling as a dry despair.
There's no way out, and no one is to blame.
Then, sharp and sweet, a sound of jazz begins
to flirt across the Thames, the pleasure boat
shines in her glass. — Slowly the music thins,
the flake of light dissolves, and a small flame
that lilted in me falters and goes out.

Plain Human

Up on this ladder, for instance,
scratching the paint away:
for what good reason? I ask myself
day after day.

Unless I maintain this property,
seal it, renew its gloss,
it can only deteriorate,
and sell at a loss.

This is important because
I've a wife and kids to support,
and they're the last people in the world
I'd wish to hurt.

I'll feed, clothe, educate;
my children in turn will marry,
learn how to wait, and go up ladders,
and scratch and worry —

so that they will be able
to feed, clothe, educate
their children, who in turn will marry
and learn to wait,

and go up ladders, of course,
and scratch and worry, so that . . .
Day after day I ask myself
precisely what

this worry-go-round is meant for;
and sometimes I look out
at the garden, which is a wilderness,
and I am caught

in a small calm of seeing:
the dustbin, perhaps, tilted
under trees at the broken fence,
light spilt

through leaves, a crimson flower
floated on air: alive
and clear in reciprocal stillnesses.
And what they have —

or what I give them, or
begin to share with them —
has nothing to do, it seems, with use
or beauty or emblem:

something to do with being
themselves. And I become
the dreamer full of discontent,
who thinks of wisdom,

solitudes, mysteries, lives
of prophets, obscure books;
the child who loved sunsets (I'm told)
and wistful nooks;

or the student who wasted time
on unprescribed authors
like Swedenborg, Boehme, the Eastern sages,
the Church Fathers;

who lagged in green retreats
to watch the mind's horizon,
or prowled the neon maze when love
secreted poison.

I have grown up since then.
Or have I? If other people
delight in working from nine to five,
are thrilled to grapple

with mortgage and hire purchase,
if it overflows the cup
of happiness to own a car,
and that's *grown up*,

well, I am still a child.
Or one of the stubborn fools
who keep on asking why and whither,
subjecting rules

to scrutiny, slipping custom.
One who can sympathize
with bums on benches, Beats on beaches
dancing to jazz,

sleeping in caves and boxes,
living on fish, avoiding
work, marrying (no strings attached)
merely by wading

into the pristine sea —
but finally aimless, caught
on the hook of the old question, flapping
like fish out of water.

'Maybe it's not the place
that matters, nor what you do',
the dreamer in me says, 'nor simply
a point of view,

but seeing, in the light
of the last analysis,
that this — the flower, the world — is so
because it's this.

Where faith coagulates,
the fears and problems tease:
we carry the why inside us
like a disease'.

Bravo: being semi-detached
instructs you how to see
hunchback and cancer victim,
beggar and refugee;

to bless the praying-mantis
munching her lover's head,
the atman of the torture cell
and the launching pad.

Figment or godlike vision,
being single it must fail
all but the crank and sage,
or petrify the will.

Plain human, I prospect
in rocky streams: let sand
bring crumbs at random, fine inklings of gold
to the weathered hand.

Music

Do I believe in marriage?
If you mean what I think you mean,
the answer must be no —
no more than I value any convention
except for its convenience.

I think the universe is
a formal creation like music,
patterns within patterns,
and that we try instinctively
to bind our own notes together:
from atoms of sound to make molecules;
from molecules, cells . . .

The bonding for social patterns is
love's valence if you're lucky,
and if you're not, affection,
pity, tolerance, justice.

Institutions are merely
names, and the names a way
of saying what people tried,
and of making rules
that first describe and then
demand the repetition of
what seemed to work best:
the man and woman bound
to their own offspring,
the dominant seventh to
the tonic triad.

But the rule-makers are always
catching up, consolidating —
after Beethoven comes
Debussy, and then Schönberg,

breaking away, creating —
and in different countries
harmonic systems differ.
So with the norms for marriage, procreation,
the bringing-up of children.

I don't believe in marriage, a mere name:
I believe in staying with
my mate and children
as long as they need or want me,
from a love or what you will
whose counterparts unite
atoms in molecules
or tones in triads —
making a social music.
Though doing it desperately
while the other half
of a double destiny loosens
the universe, and all that's made
suffers a slow corrosion.

1 : Standing Water

Ironist now, equilibrist, I was
a hero then — the salt a sailor's wit,
a winedark leaping lustre, supple, taut,
spuming beneath the wind; and heroes' laws
were elemental rhythm — no human thought
to clip the dream, to make the passion fit.
I used to marvel as I watched the ship
slicing luminous fathoms: she would dip
and rise, alive and shuddering on a will
that chose the meaning for her, by dominion
freed her from the exigencies of freedom —
its power, acknowledged, then most prodigal.

Agents of destiny, we chose the means
but not the meaning: primal opposites
involved us in their greatness as we manned
the fateful seesaw. Now, both rise
and fall forsake me. Landlubber, prudent king,
diplomat, man of means, with time to think,
compelled to choose a meaning I devise
these ironies that bring
contraries into temper: choose, in fact,
the mean — for we are human. This is not
despair, extremity — since rise and fall
forsake me now: when life and death contract,
when water stands, both are impossible.
This mood is but the fog and stink of meanness,
miasma of the deadlife, meaning's rot.

2 : Wounds

A blank, like this.
Fog muffling the shore,
a tedium of sand,
the trite conforming pebbles.
Only the sea's hiss
reminds me of its roar.
A salt memory troubles
wounds that will not heal.
The spent wave whispers
Odysseus, now you feel
the salt rubbed in, the lost
leap of the sea transmuted.
Who sailed to islands, kissed
Calypso once, and knew
the taste of salt leaping,
safe in his kingdom drew
a blank, a wet mist
on grey shingle weeping.

3 : Calypso

Crazed by the suck and roar
of spinning water — nine days
clear of the drowned — tugged from a lurching spar,
flopped like a seal where waves elide and glaze
warm sand, I came ashore.
The sailor found his woman standing there.

Firelight on hair and skin; a scent
of smoke from cedar logs and pepperwood.
She called me and I went,
making no choice of bad or good:
whatever choosing meant,
only the girl, half goddess, understood.

The coiled sea takes us in.
Freeing ourselves we bind ourselves:
doing what we need, we do what must be done.
The cone of darkness fills as it revolves,
lifts us out into the foaming sun.
Climactic water swills the jagged shelves.

The crusts of fire flake down: a red spark
dissolves in moonlight . . . Dawn, the slow
focusing of rock where four streams play
beneath a vine; deep woods for owl and crow,
clear of the filtered dark.
A trance of distance sublimates the bay

to a thin sift of thunder . . .
After such nights, such days. At first,
leaving her there asleep, I used to wander
back to the crude source, where combers burst
spilling white grains of water,
and squealing gulls — touched nerves in the wind —

were twinges of sharp lust.
Both day and night, it seemed, were provident,
reciprocal as host and guest.
And yet the idyll faltered, the enchantment
left something over, grit of discontent:
the innocence of dawn became a cyst.

Hunched in the cool dark one afternoon,
I heard Calypso singing while she wove –
her body, in the opening of the cave,
edged with a down of light. Perhaps the tune,
the blonde hair brimming over in the sun,
a movement, or some old domestic flavour

tricked me – or indeed
I solved an absence by telepathy,
from the deep shafts of truth a slighted need
drew substance: but I saw Penelope
there, in an arched radiance, and she made
from whispering spools a web of loyalty.

The dour eroding pain
grown harsh, I left the cave,
clambered through wind that sawed against the grain
of gnarled blue water; in the grumbling cove
loitered all afternoon,
hearing the shingle rasp, the gulls complain.

Perhaps desire and guilt
grinding together, or the lie
that strikes through self-fulfilment, a rock's fault.
On jagged shelves the leaping foam gives way
in slack pools, finally in grains, a dry
precipitate, the irony of salt.

4 : The Web

Alone under the sky, the horizon our only limit —
never limiting but always moving away, granting
something to move towards, and space to move in
that never stopped being distance until the skyline
was rock that stayed put (though landfall meant
freedom too, actions worth travelling for) —
we were the few for whom the sea was woven.

I stand now on the cliffs on a summer day.
White clouds accumulate above the horizon,
whose tempered edge stays put, and bounds a space
empty of ships. With a pretence of meaning
the water glides towards me in shining folds —
is chafed and slashed, ravels on black stone.
There is no meaning here: I have none to give.

My home, my island kingdom: in bays and inlets
the spent sea scuffs, kicking the driftwood idly.
I climb through drowsy air: voices of bee and cricket
float on the gulls' cries. In a nest of bracken
I see a silky cone, as though a tunnel
of spun smoke, delicate and exact —
and deep inside, patient as death, the spider.

5 : Special Pleading

Even now, so long after my return,
she weeps despairingly some days, thinking
of how the past violated the future,
trying to understand. For me, in a sense,
there was nothing to understand but being a man
who voyages far from home, elate with searching;
but nothing I say dissolves her metaphor
of the needling worm, the fruit brown and pulpy
losing its grip. She attacks, and pity grows
a steel point of guilt: in self-defence
I stab, and then regret. The killer's love
makes murder suicide. And not to die —
sailor at heart, sickening of government —
I plead there are salt reaches woven, unravelled,
woven again by the world's generous rhythm;
and proud sorrowful hands unpicking truth
for virtue's sake, craftily, night by night.

'Can you imagine what it did to me,
that long torment of belief and doubt? —
how I grew sick of drudging day and night,
of lying alone, watching the blank sea,
hearing the drunken suitors brag and fight,
afraid some bitch would let the secret out.

P for Penelope, and pure, and prude:
the choice of words could sting, but made known
the speaker's heart, not mine. How many read
truly the cipher of my solitude?
Which of them would have fondled me in bed
to give me pleasure, not to steal a throne?

I was not pure, nor prudish: there were nights
I longed to do what other women do,
afflicted with a sweet insanity
that fashioned gods even from parasites.
It wasn't fear, or shame, or vanity
restrained me then, but somehow, loving you'.

7 : *Up to a Point*

How are we different then?
If this is Love
that pairs a wife with other men
in fancy, but in deed
preserves her for a husband's need —
as though a glove

could fit no hand but one —
Love is too dim
to understand what men have done:
I'd rather hear you say
we're friends, lascivious and gay:
let's pension him.

And then the way is clear
to wonder why
your will, if not in shame or fear,
could hold, and mine slip
like driftwood from the weir's lip,
no longer I.

What makes a man destroy
all gentle thought,
turn killer in the streets of Troy
or sweat in Circe's bed?
Self-will, the moralists have said;
but I have caught

a stranger meaning there:
that when the will
pierces to remote air,
ascending like a stone
whose arc implies how it was thrown,
it soars until

an infinitely small
articulation
ease its thrusting to a fall.
Dark causes that direct
self-will, accomplish their effect
by self-negation.

What cloth can match the weave
of right and wrong?
Hurled stones — you felt in make-believe
a lover's hands, and I
was drawn like any traveller by
Calypso's song.

But somehow you were still
yourself — had stopped
in time the soaring thrust of will —
when mine had reached the crest
and touched a needle point of rest
before it dropped.

8: *The Singers*

The logs crack and flare.
Each night the story tellers dream
and lightly
pluck their harps and sing,
praising a wife's care,
a fearless king.
And we who are their theme
listen politely.

Deceivers who have no
alternative, we let the myth
grow stronger.
The divided air
resumed its single flow,
but now we share
what death has tampered with,
a love no longer

filling canvas, fresh
with salt. Hearing the words float
on wonder,
trying to know the god
grained in the mortal flesh,
you see blood
spurt from a slashed throat,
and rape, and plunder;

spent killers after war
hungry for sex, grown tired of ships
and danger,
debauched in some glazed island
by drug pedlar and whore;
the wasting husband,
new salt upon his lips,
come home a stranger.

What lies they tell to make
ideal truth! No false relations
tangle
this music combed from harps,
though women lie awake
and love warps,
and partners sworn to patience
fret and wrangle.

Heroic tempers brood
in the after-calm, as sultry air
forebodes
violence. We have no
healing from solitude
when in the slow
acid of your despair
a dream corrodes.

9: Dream and Reality

In the estuary the fresh and the salt mingle.
Her supple calms beneath the noon sun
glide on shingle, flicker with thorned light.
In a translucent haze, bulged waters run
smoothly between the headlands. — Not where grinding
fathoms crumble the bones of lost ships,
or clinking brooks are winding amidst granite,
but where the markets hum and the galley dips
creaking along the wharf in a stink of tar,
life proves the grain of wisdom, and we learn
humanity. The spar, the drowned man, deep
in a groiling cone of violence, turn and turn:
in the spun pool of frenzy a hero's will
founders: whose rage cries out? whose arm jags
the blade home, swills the Trojan ground with blood?
But here men watch the tide: their net swags
its load of rinsed silver across the gunnel;
others bake bread, construct in marble, crush
the grape for sweet runnels of wine, fill
their water skins where cold shallows flush
on pebbles, dump cedar logs that cough
a golden spindrift under the fat cauldron,
lead cattle to the trough. Still lovers hate,
and parents fight an absurd war with children;
a rival is broken or a friend betrayed;
by misadventure, suicide, disease,
Death's fortune is made. The people curse
and weep and go on living: by degrees
the balance levels, tilts the other way
with dancing and making love and the pride of skill.
I've watched the numb grey of *meden agan*
burn as the golden mean when heart and will
have coupled. Residual passion stirs in dreams
and legends, from whose dark truth are drawn
blinding extremes that flare in the mind's mirror

but, freed from distance, outrage human law —
rive the tough grain, leaving it scorched and brittle.
Alone in the noon silence I look down
at the estuary, the little streets and buildings,
the sea cutting blue notches in the town —
inland the glancing torrents and the groves,
and where the waves pound, headlands dividing
gull-flaked coves, thinning away like echoes,
and heaped with immense clouds the ocean sliding
godly across the world: calm vision makes
one harmony of the disparate, but we live
where wholeness breaks, where objects, qualities,
beliefs and feelings are competitive —
but then defined reciprocally, as though
a kind of love made difference possible,
or difference a kind of love. And we grow human
where opposites are poised, made workable,
where salt and fresh merge at the river's end.
The task of hermit or of hero feeds
on energies that transcend the human will,
yet has for origin the same needs
as those that keep this little town alert,
edgy, tenacious — where, though difference
intensified can hurt, becoming conflict,
passion releases no such violence
as ravaged in the howling streets of Troy.
But black shadows are made by brilliant light:
deep joy involves deep sorrow, people say,
remembering those whose fortune was to fight
human tyranny, natural disaster —
festering heroes, layabouts, war bores
bogged in the past, drinking themselves to death.
Yet many have come to terms, outgrown the whores
in foreign seaports, camaraderie, total
discipline that absolved them from the need
to think, and the brutal ecstasy of killing:
these are the ones I search — not those who bleed

memories in the pubs — for signs of pain,
and then of joy: veterans who came home
and took the strain of being entirely human.
In firelight the harp glissandos run like foam
from bows that slice green water: I watch the eyes
dreaming, think how the floated words tell
true lies, shaping, distancing all that lures
the mind to make a fact of heaven or hell —
difference intensified, the fresh and salt
unmingled, hero's rage and hermit's trance.
A rock's fault . . . Slowly the wound heals,
the severed strata knit: and in the glance
of women who for parched years were still
themselves, grass-widowed while their husbands learned
to gallivant and kill, experience lights
a penetrating love, where the old burned
wistful in bland wax. My dreams contain
the truth of primal opposites; in the common
I seek their strong blend, the truly sane:
Penelope and Calypso in one woman.

Freud

When did you hear me say
'Now that you know
what forces are at play,
you must let go,
and on the dark tide
of a violent age
drift into suicide'?

I did not teach despair,
but how it could be defeated
by fact and order. Beware
the cry of the Zeitgeist-monger;
all history can swerve
to the pull of one man's hunger —
and sick minds can be treated.

Gospel Town

Under its hump the town
endures nightfall. Sand
sweats as the tide uncovers
drainage and slimy stone.
Fairylights, fountain, bandstand
play the uneasy lovers.

Their ingrown hungers rage:
hot sermons, anodyne
of hymns, disturb the patter
of the hypnotist on the stage,
where tranced lips guzzle wine
from glasses filled with water.

Pure streams from granite ledges
fall through the glens, and swill
flat shingle solitudes
beyond the last bridges.
Unfathomably still
the black mountain broods.

The Undertow

What is it sets the alarm
to drill me at six-thirty,
impels me away from home
and across the city,
defined by the suit I keep
for occasions? What is it tries
to drag me back to sleep,
dulling my eyes,
wanting the other to steer
clear and leave me alone?
Why do I turn the fear
to a skin of ice, a stone
crust on the quick of magma?
I arrive at a box of glass
as cold as dogma;
no whisper of trees, no grass:
man is the spearhead now.
What thrusts me into this room
where they offer no welcome, bow
over documents, exhume
my past, rummage and prod,
shoot questions at me like
a firing squad,
or turn me on a spike
over their singeing scorn?
'Thank you' . . . In the street
I feel my roots torn
for building, am obsolete
as greenness. But trees rejoice —
not I: before I started
something had made a choice
and left me heavy-hearted,
reluctant, turning in.
Survival says I should be
content to have saved my skin —

licking my wounds, but free
of the specialists branching towards
extinction: the one who found
his hands and a gift for words.
But I wince at the drilling sound:
it jags in me like a knife.
You tried the flowers, the birds,
the gnat and the dinosaur:
which candidate now, dear life?
Where are you heading for?

Open to the Public

After four centuries – from the dirt
grand patrons dwindled to – merchants and plebs
reverse their destiny at the clicking stile.
Into an ancient calm the children blurt,
where leisured paths wander and cattle graze.
The lake prickles with sunlight, and a mile
of foliage cools the summer in green webs.

The mansion from its legendary haze
emerges hard and white. Respectful clods,
we climb the steps, enter the Great Hall.
Hushed voices echo; a subtle brilliance plays
on bronze and marble. Eros and Apollo,
immured with Cicero and the Dying Gaul,
are stone-cold dreams who once were living gods.

Adagio from room to room we follow
the guidebook through an intricate décor
of gold and peacock, walnut, stucco, silk.
Some say magnificent, and others hollow;
a few say Robert Adam and look wise.
The youngsters grouch, a baby squalls for milk;
two schoolboys, tired of art, are playing war.

This grandeur was a politician's prize,
its history laced with blood. First Somerset,
then Simple Tom the Martyr, lost their heads,
and Cruel Henry in a warp of spies
coughed on a musket ball. Here Cromwell honed
the steel that left a monarchy in shreds,
and love turned violent in a widow's net.

Death claimed his revenue, the proud atoned
for daring to possess; then duke and duchess,
marrying peace and comfort with renown,

were free to cherish gaily what they owned —
had pipers and Swiss porters, worked the land,
renewed a structure and a style, till Brown
and Adam put the last beguiling touches:

where lilies float, two lovers hand in hand
gaze on the water they are pictured in,
and dark things are transfigured as they were
when blades and virgins danced the saraband.
Softly the polished ivy hugs the tree,
the belladonna makes a drowsy stir,
and a clear sky dissolves the peregrine.

At the old riding-school they serve a tea
of buttered toast and scones and cherry cake.
Sparrows from airy rafters dive for crumbs,
a royal coach displays its pedigree:
and dilettanti calling up the past
omit the slopping guts, the mashed thumbs,
and courtly rascals mirrored in the lake.

The little patrons — raw, but learning fast —
retire and leave this glory to the dark.
In terraces and flats the pride of kings
inches like mercury: half iconoclast
and half creator, life through arc on arc
moves endlessly — and leaves among the things
it lavished at the crest, this lovely park.

Five Foot Ten

Among the drooping plants
a few green hairs
on a dry scalp of mud
itchy with ants,
their trickling multitude
busy with great affairs.

Each tiny street
fidgets and effervesces
with two-way traffic. They meet
head on, avoid with slick
footwork collision and loss.
But social stresses

erupt in frenzied wars:
they squirt and pinch
in twos and then in dozens,
their highways inch by inch
glutted with scores
of slaughtered citizens.

Inside a lens
only the scale alters:
proportion is the same
between intelligence
and the achieved aim.
A different need filters

pain and aspiration
into the crystal jars
of love and art and god,
whose distillation
spills from the smashed beauty
among the brains and blood.

One world, an equal right
to live, for ants and men.
One irony of *us*
or them: one need to fight.
They're small but numerous;
we're few, but five foot ten.

My life must act, being theirs.
Gigantic, swift, I raise
the kettle: they had their chances.
While that which makes me human —
my pitying heart — delays,
the lethal fluid pounces.

Metamorphoses

In blocks of serpentine
polished for generations
by families going down to Kynance Cove,
the coloured minerals tangle veins as fine
as threads, like intricate decorations.
Charmed by their loveliness,
the shine of August, waves on smooth sand,
how could we think of metamorphic stress,
of burning fluids that wove
the subtle characters we tread,
in whose complexities each delicate strand
shows how the earth bled —
or, among swimsuits, towels, suntan lotion,
slipping off shirts and frocks
where long ago magmatic waters drained,
and seeing the compulsive ocean
carve what those trickling fires engrained,
read our own birth and shaping in the rocks?

Mysterious fragments — so the cliff dreams —
shine on the littoral that was forming here
like a crude prototype of bone
when salty shallows coupling with the wind
conceived the biosphere:
with colours purer than its own —
a mineral vision dancing in the bay —
empyrean satin gleams
on bodies tender, golden-skinned,
that blur in bright obscurities of spray
and come forth radiant still.
But neither rock nor breaker shares
with man the double will
he seeks where only energies can be —
while a curt rubric on the tideline spells
changes as natural as theirs:

46

windless, the living fires go out, and cells
are broken down like crystals in the sea.

But who should think of death
on such a day, in such a place as this,
where everything perceived can be enjoyed:
guests of the green ocean, drawing breath
from the same wind, and noticing perhaps
with what an easy grace two youngsters kiss,
white girl and coloured boy — how they avoid,
coming on truth instinctively, the traps
of superstition — we might have thought rather
that wholeness and diversity generate
the only love the world has ever known,
that differences belong to one another:
reciprocal the forms of cliff and sea,
the little points and lines flecking the stone,
the people and their races. But only we —
who feel distinctions, having minds and hearts --
can love, trying to see the whole, or hate,
insisting on the parts.

From sinuous intrusions
weaving the colours of the serpentine,
to the spun chromosomes prefiguring
the nerve cells of a son and daughter
delighted by a pebble, everything
is change: to make and to destroy
lose meaning in the rich confusions
of chance or infinite design.
And yet at Kynance Cove, seeing a boy
beaten against the cliff — but not by water:
by a man's will and sinew —
and thinking how the tide of kinship runs
compulsively, and of the neural stress
that sparks all human sorrows, angers, fears,

47

I wept for differences. In rage of guns
primordial fires continue:
but magma, though hell-hot, is passionless,
and the salt streams on rocks were never tears.

The Veteran

One of the lucky ones,
I do what I can.
Chatting, reading the news
to an old disabled man,
I wonder how
he stays in his right mind,
so much of his world is dead.
He faced the guns
at Ypres, was gassed and sent
to this very ward where now —
lacking his left eye,
in the other almost blind,
with an arm he cannot use,
legs damaged, a tube to drain
his bladder, a little bag
of urine at his thigh —
once more he sits in bed,
endures the long drag
of time without event,
the slow corrosive pain.

The first time he said 'sir',
hearing the way I spoke,
it made me wince, and then
was touching and amusing —
as though I were
a young padre diffusing
good cheer among the men.
Being treated so, in view of
his eighty years and all
he'd seen of life and death,
was quite a joke.
Sometimes he would recall
the things I only knew of
from text or photograph,

and now the thin breath
that whistles in his throat,
the clouded eye, the grey
cadaverous face,
remind me every day
of how he bled
once in a remote
time, a remote place,
and has been living half
a century with the dead.

Dolores

A little girl who survived a firing squad 32 years ago, but who has been in a coma ever since, died today.

(Newspaper report, 1968)

Thirty two years ago,
shifting the corpses for burial,
they found her underneath
still breathing.

The bullet drawn,
her delicate flesh made whole,
she slept through the long maturing
of child and maid and woman.

Her blood ran evenly, her brain
lived on when her mind stopped:
form without meaning,
a name for no one.

Lying alone
deep in the snarled growth
of rose and lily,
she had one gift at least:

if love, searching, torn
on briars, was almost there,
and would have kissed her wide awake
to the last blaze of childhood —

her mother's weeping,
her father's hard silence,
the dreadful intimation (worse
than nightmares or being lost)

when suddenly all the rifles
pointed one way, demanding
her four simple years —
she died before it reached her.

51

Integration

Suddenly I heard squeals
echoing under the bridge. Beside the water
this dog at his mistress' heels
came slouching. My little daughter
ran to the safety of my arm
and huddled there,
staring. 'He won't do you any harm'
I said. A moment later
it was my turn to stare.

A mongrel: its body a stodged
Alsatian, the head thickened;
its face, abrupt as a mask under
a sooty streak of hair, some kind
of terrier. Passing us, it dodged
furtively, long tail wilting, to skulk behind
protective legs. For a moment I felt sickened
as if by a cruel joke, or at best a blunder
due to an absent mind.

Yet mixtures are common enough:
in art, in people and animals, flowers and metals,
old jealousies compromise,
and unities die in the heterogeneous stuff
to make fresh unities. Custom smooths
a gravelling image; in the eyes
of the dazed beholder beauty settles,
as though a riddle were solved, or lies
turned themselves into truths.

The shock of novelty then.
Or could it be one of those
disparities that forever outrun
the stride of the human mind,

like the hippo bulking on tiny trotters, men
savaging what they love, or the sun
killing the root with kindness? Terrier's nose,
Alsatian's rump: to whoever, whatever designed
the multifarious world it is all one.

The River

The content of a river is
its form, its form the water
which is the river. The river is itself.
Not water simply,
but water folded, curled
exactly thus and now . . . and now . . . and now:
tugged smooth on clenched knuckles,
a skin of oiled light
sleeking off rock; the smash
of dumped foam; gold lenses over gravel.

Each detail is itself,
exactly here and now. Inventing space:
no edge of water fines to definition,
the split hair splits — but nowhere, being here,
masses and shines like water.
Inventing time: this now
was then — the split second
split to infinity — yet now or never
evolves the racing water,
whose planes are stillness gliding off a spool.

Each clear identity is so because
all are reciprocal: this rock, this water
not simply that, but rock being smoothed by water,
and water honed on rock.
But with no here and now, unless
everywhere, always: each immeasurable,
all therefore simply this. Without these shapes,
themselves, there is no river; without the river,
nothing. The river is the form,
the form the content. The content is itself.

Pigeons

They paddle with staccato feet
in powder-pools of sunlight,
small blue busybodies
strutting like fat gentlemen
with hands clasped
under their swallowtail coats;
and as they stump about,
their heads like tiny hammers
tap at imaginary nails
in non-existent walls.

Elusive ghosts of sunshine
slither down the green gloss
of their necks an instant, and are gone.

Summer hangs drugged from sky to earth
in limpid fathoms of silence:
only warm dark dimples of sound
slide like slow bubbles
from the contented throats.

Raise a casual hand —
with one quick gust
they fountain into air.

(1946)